REA

11·28·19

KRIS KRISTOFFERSON

KRIS KRISTOFFERSON

by Beth Kalet

quick fox

New York · London · Tokyo

Copyright © Quick Fox 1979

All rights reserved.

International Standard Book Number: ISBN: 0-8256-3932-8

Library of Congress Catalog Card Number: 79-63528

Printed in the United States of America.

In Great Britain: Book Sales Ltd.,
78 Newman Street, London W1P 3LA, England

In Canada: Gage Trade Publishing,
P.O. Box 5000, 164 Commander Blvd.,
Agincourt, Ontario M1S 3C7, Canada

In Japan: Music Sales Corporation,
4-26-22 Jingumae, Shibuya-ku,
Tokyo 150, Japan

Designed by Jacques Chazaud

Front cover photograph   by Mark Sennet

Back cover photograph   courtesy of Hy Simon

Typeset by Filmar Graphics, Inc., San Diego, CA

INTRODUCTION

He possesses a raw masculine aura that makes him at once a man's man and a woman's dream. His presence is electric. His intense crystal blue eyes penetrate, they tell the stories he sings. His tousled brown hair (now with a few sexy strands of gray) frames his face alluringly. Onstage, he appears as a cowboy who might have been born in the faded Levis and western shirt that so becomes him.

This is Kris Kristofferson, the real man and not a purposely created image. It is his inimitable charisma that has drawn his features into an image, and as happens with stars, it is his image that represents him to his audiences.

This gorgeous, straightforward man, now in his middle years, is wrapped in incongruity. His easy good looks, rough accent, and suggestive honey and hickory voice belie the depth of a man who has always chosen the hardest paths and attained his goals, who has studied English literature at Oxford, flown helicopters in the Army, and written some of Nashville's classic songs.

When fans see Kris Kristofferson, they see a star — a man at the top of the heap, who has become an enormously successful songwriter, singer, and actor. Some fans put their stars on pedestals and create larger than life images which they insist the stars must live up to. Fans can negate a star's individuality. Getting to the top is no small accomplishment; staying there is even tougher. The pedestal, instead of being a reward for hard work and a job well done, becomes an albatross, because a star must live up to his fans' image of him rather than fulfill his own expectations. Kris Kristofferson has avoided this trap.

Many rock critics have viewed Kris only from a rock perspective, expecting each song he writes to be as monumental and universal as "Me & Bobby McGee."

But to categorize Kris would be unfair. He is essentially a country writer. He has worked within the traditional country framework and expanded it beyond its former limitations, allowing it to encompass subjects, feelings, and ideas which had previously been considered taboo in country. More than anyone else, Kris Kristofferson has been credited with affecting a dramatic change in country music. Yet, he no more fits the country mold than he does the rock mold.

Country enthusiasts like their heroes to be the sorts of fellows who are given to fits of rambunctiousness, who have had their share of hard times, possibly brushed with the law, and gone through a divorce or two. While only certain aspects of this description may fit Kris, he has been plagued with this sort of an image.

Kris wishes to be taken for what he is. He doesn't put on airs. He makes mistakes, questions his actions and abilities, and changes his mind. He continues to grow and learn from all his experiences. He is serious and sarcastic; he is a thinker and also whimsical; he is a man with a deep family commitment, an ever-broadening career, and, on top of it all, he is one of our stars.

Kris' rise to the top has not been easy. It was not so long ago that he was living in a $50-a-month tenement in Nashville, working as a janitor in Columbia studios, and trying to peddle his songs to the bigwigs in country music.

Recently, Kris overheard a man on a plane say about him, "God, he's got so much charisma!" "Godalmighty!" Kris exclaimed, "Where the hell was all the charisma all those years I was a janitor? Why the hell didn't nobody say: 'That kid sweepin' floors, he's got charisma, put him on stage!' The only charisma I've got is the one you-all put there. I'm the same guy I always was."

Kris' success in Nashville has been extraordinary. His songs stand now as true country classics and seem to have risen from the soul of country. Three of his most popular songs, "Me & Bobby McGee," "Sunday Mornin' Comin' Down," and "Help Me Make It Through The Night," are perennial country anthems, sensitively reflecting on the dreams and realities of living.

But for years Kris peddled these songs to country singers, hoping they would record them, and for years these same songs were turned down because they were too emotional, too intellectual and too risqué. In the interim, while Kris lived hand to mouth, sweeping floors, tending bar, and digging ditches, he sacrificed a great deal besides comfort. Because he was determined to make song-writing his career, he suffered tremendous personal losses, the greatest of which were the esteem of his family and the breakup of his marriage.

1976 *UPI*

HIS CHILDHOOD, SCHOOL YEARS, OXFORD

Kristoffer Kristofferson was born on June 22, 1937, in Brownsville, Texas, where he spent the majority of his childhood. Because of his father's military career, the family, (his sister Karen, now married to an Army officer, and brother Craig, now a Navy jet pilot,) moved from town to town across the country. Kris, while becoming a well-traveled youth, earned the title of "Army brat." His family life was comfortable; his father was a very successful man, and his parents hoped that Kris would follow in his footsteps, perhaps with an Army career. None of the Kristofferson children had to work as teens, but Kris did. He spent his summers working various jobs including working with labor crews and with fire-fighting gangs in Alaska.

Kris has always been an unusual person. He has always had interests and desires different from the crowd, even when he was very popular. Growing up in Brownsville, Texas, all the kids listened to Patti Page and Johnny Ray, but Kris' musical tastes were considered weird by his peers; he was crazy about Hank Williams. Early on, Kris decided that he would be a songwriter. Knowing that his dad, an Air Force Major General, wouldn't approve, Kris told him that he was planning to become a writer. He knew that his father would imagine him sitting behind a desk, smoking a pipe, and wearing a tweed jacket with suede elbow patches — a respectable image for a career military man to have of his son.

Shortly before Kris was of high school age, the family moved to San Mateo, California, in the San Francisco Bay area, and Kris went to San Mateo High. Kris was a model student, which pleased his parents immensely. While his interests in writing and music continued to be mainstays in his life, he was also active in football. Kris felt that by being a football star he could find another outlet for his deep feelings of "separation," as he has since put it. By playing football well, he distinguished himself from the crowd, achieved a distance, and made his individuality known. He tried unsuccessfully to win football scholarships to

1971 *UPI*

Dartmouth and Yale, and eventually decided on attending Pomona College, a fine, though small liberal arts school in southern California.

At Pomona, Kris easily distinguished himself in a tremendous variety of ways. He played football and won conference recognition as an end; boxed Golden Gloves; organized a rugby team; and as testament to his athletic prowess, was featured in a *Sports Illustrated* article. He was president of his freshman and sophomore classes, and as a creative writing major, became president of the debating team and the writing club. Kris was the top-rated ROTC cadet, and was platoon commander. "I was the worst platoon commander that school ever saw; I could never give a guy a demerit," he says. And, quite naturally, he was the most popular boy in school. If all this activity sounds foreign to today's students, remember Kris went to college in the mid-fifties, and that was a bit before the upheavel of the 60's and the subsequent apathetic 70's.

One former classmate felt that Kris was so popular he could have become President, right then and there, if he had wanted to. But, he also recalls, that there was always something inside of Kris that made him unsettled, unhappy, and a person no one could really get to know.

Kris knew that he wanted to be a writer. He looked on writing as his special way of distinguishing himself, of expressing his feelings, and of working out problems. He was a gifted writer, and as he later proved, could use words to express new meanings. He entered the prestigious *Atlantic Monthly* magazine's national collegiate short story contest and won the top four out of twenty prizes. With this encouragement, Kris started his first novel with the intention of becoming a novelist.

Perhaps the tweed-jacketed, pipe-smoking writer was an image that Kris himself rather liked. At any rate, his writing abilities had been recognized, and his future in the field looked promising. At the end of his tenure at Pomona, Kris was awarded a Phi Beta Kappa key and was recommended for and won a Rhodes Scholarship to study English literature at Merton College, Oxford University.

Kris says that he went off to Oxford a "star" and quickly discovered that he wasn't. The British, he says, have a way of cutting through layers of pretense. His situation at Oxford was tenuous. He immersed himself in his literature studies, but didn't get along well with the other literature students. They seemed to look down their noses at him, treating him as an uncultured fool. In part, his own obstinancy was the cause of this problem, making him an outsider on much of the Oxford scene. Students addressed him dismissively as "Tex" or "Yank" and so, characteristically, he clung to his accent all the more, refusing to pick up any of the British influence in his speech. His studies at Oxford went along fine, however, and one of his

Newport Folk Festival, 1969   *David Gahr*

teachers claimed that he was "one of the most favorable specimens of Rhodes Scholarship." Kris had become very involved in the 18th century British poet and engraver William Blake, and he found an endless source of inspiration in his writings. "Blake opened up doors for me . . . that old dead poet."

Today, Kris is still very much a student of Blake, finding ways to bring him up in nearly every interview he gives.

If his rapport with Oxford's scholarly community was not great, he made up for it with his rapport with the athletic community. He resumed his boxing and won a blue ribbon, but he wasn't even allowed to try out for the rugby team, even though he had organized Pomona's team, because the English felt that an American couldn't know anything about the game. Still, he found the athletes to be more his type.

It was at this time that Kris began a singularly distinguished pursuit for an Oxford student. Along with his athletic endeavors, his studies, and his novel, Kris had been writing songs, as he had been doing since he was eleven years old. His first song, entitled "I Hate Your Ugly Face" (to the best of his memory) was a direct imitation of Hank Williams' style. But at Oxford, Kris' song-writing took on a style of its own — a folksy-bluesy style, easy to hear and understand, and pleasant to listen to. Already apparent was Kris' ability to turn phrases around in order to present duality — a hallmark of his writing today. Kris knew how to make reversals work effectively.

One day Kris saw an ad in London's *Daily Mirror* addressed to young musicians which invited them to "Just Dial FAME." He took the ad to heart and met Paul Lincoln, a Soho coffee bar owner who had been gathering talented young musicians, performers, and writers, and was the man behind England's successful entertainer Tommy Steele. Lincoln heard tapes of Kris singing and playing his songs and quickly signed him up. Kris then began, in addition to his studies, singing in Soho and it seemed that he was on his way to becoming a star at the tender age of twenty-two. Unfortunately, as time would prove, it wasn't until eleven years later that Kris would realize this dream.

In 1959, Kris, who resembled Ricky Nelson with a slightly pudgy face, crew-cut hair, and quite amiable boyish features, began a short-lived career as Kris Carson. He signed a contract with the British recording firm Top Rank and immediately set off with a carload of friends to vacation in Switzerland using the first of his earnings. His goal then, as later in his early Nashville days, was to be able to make enough money to support himself while writing.

His fame, small as it was, spread across the Atlantic in a brief article in *Time* magazine under the "Education" heading, which put it this way: "Kristofferson is in a fair way to become wealthy as a teenager's guitar-thwonking singing idol." The article also interviewed Kris' Merton College tutor Hugo Dyson (the same man who said Kris was one of "the most favorable specimens of Rhodes Scholarship") as to whether he felt Kris would give up his studies in literature for a career in singing. Dyson was quoted as saying that Kris was "the kind of man you can trust to pick his own career."

THE MILITARY

Kris received a degree in English literature from Oxford and was scheduled to continue his studies there, but during a Christmas break spent at home in California, he decided not to return to Oxford.

While at home, Kris had begun seeing an old high school girlfriend, Fran Beir, and they were married. In retrospect, Kris says that they thought they could solve each other's problems. It was about this time, and for the next several years, that Kris found himself at a low point in his enthusiasm, his writing, and his self-respect.

Two publishers had asked to see his completed manuscripts, and he thought that this would be his big break, that his dream of becoming a novelist was about to be realized. When his work was rejected, he felt depressed and questioned his abilities. His despair sent him into a long period of depression, and he wasn't sure of what he should do next. Then, Fran became pregnant, and Kris was suddenly thrust into the position of breadwinner. He was at a low point of self-confidence, and not knowing what else to do, he joined the Army. Though he knew it meant putting off his dreams of becoming a writer; at the time he felt it was all he could do. He never looked on the service as a career, only as a stop-gap measure.

His family was rather proud of him, thinking that he was about to begin a dazzling military career as his father had. But Kris hated filling out forms, hated training camp, and hated the regimentation of Army life. The military, though, was good to him. He went to jump school, to flight school, and became a pilot. "I hated the Army, but I loved flying," Kris said, and he rose quickly up the ranks, becoming an *extremely* young captain.

Kris did his entire tour (4½ years) in Germany flying helicopters. In this respect he was lucky, because his family could be with him. He and Fran and their daughter lived in one Army town after another, moving from one furnished room to another. During this time, Kris felt that he'd touched bottom. He hadn't written anything in a long time; being in the military

Monticello Race Track, 1972 *Chuck Pulin*

stifled him, and his own lack of self-respect didn't arouse his creativity. He began to drink heavily (a habit that stayed with him for many years); more often than not he was drunk, and in general, he was feeling depressed. One augmented the other — drinking, depression, and lack of creativity. He wanted nothing less than to be an Army man, but he just couldn't seem to get his creativity going.

During this "low" period, Kris totalled two cars and had four motorcycle accidents. He still doesn't like to deal with cars, he says. This recklessness, he feels, was attributable to his drinking and his being down on himself.

In about his third year in Germany, Kris got together with a few of the guys he worked with and formed a band which played at clubs for enlisted men and non-commissioned officers. This activity made him feel a great deal better, and he resumed his songwriting. A friend, another helicopter pilot, suggested that he send some of his material to a relative in Nashville, Marijohn Wilkin, songwriter, publisher, and writer of "Long Black Veil."

Marijohn Wilkin wrote back that when he returned to the States, Kris should stop by to see her. That encouragement was enough.

Shortly thereafter, Kris had been assigned to return to the States to take a position teaching literature at West Point. He had a two-week leave between assignments, and irrationally, instead of going home, he went directly to Nashville, still in uniform. He struck a strange picture there, short-haired, shy, and awed at the goings-on of Music City. People on the streets called him captain and saluted him as he walked by. He was determined to see Marijohn Wilkin, however, and to see Nashville, the home of country music.

His meeting with Marijohn Wilkin was not especially encouraging, as she was not anxious to press Kris to try his luck in Nashville, knowing just how hard it really is to make it there. Kris did manage to meet Johnny Cash briefly, a man who later had a tremendous influence on Kris' spirit and career, as well as a few other of Nashville's stars. He was so enamored of the excitement of the lifestyle that he stayed there for his entire two-week leave, and was so taken by the spirit of Nashville that he wrote seven songs. Kris said that Nashville encouraged him to write. He could see stories everywhere, and he thought that if he didn't make it as a songwriter, he could continue his literary pursuits there because ideas seemed to jump up at him from every corner.

Kris returned home long enough to have his orders changed, thereby managing to extricate himself from his Army entanglements, grab his wife and daughter, and return to Nashville. Fran was scared, but she came with him. Her only experience with the music business was Kris' rag-tag band in

UNICEF Show, 1979   *Hy Simon*

the Army; it's doubtful that her first Nashville experiences were any more reassuring.

She had seen him through his darkest Army days, when his drinking was perhaps the only constant in his life, and now she set off with him on this new, and highly doubtful, venture. Kris' family was appalled at this latest career decision of his and had little correspondence with him at first. They had thought that he would follow an Army career and were extremely disappointed with his irrational move to Nashville. His father had been a success, and at the time, it was asking too much of his family to understand, no less that they foresee that this move would prove as right as it did. He had always followed the prescribed paths and excelled at everything he did, but this was a switch — to knowingly place himself into abject poverty, coupled with the less than respectable nature (in their eyes) of trying to make it as a songwriter, was simply more than they could handle.

Another bleak, yet productive period of Kris' life began.

A Star Is Born *Frank Edwards/Fotos International*

1970   *Pictorial Parade*

Rita Coolidge   1974   *Frank Edwards/Fotos International*

THE NASHVILLE STRUGGLE

Kris and Fran rented a $50-a-month cold water flat and set up "housekeeping." His intention at this point was to use as much of his time as possible to write and to try to sell his songs. He had no desire to record his own material, but instead hoped to write for other country singers. To this end, he held a number of poor-paying jobs, including tending bar, digging ditches, and working as a janitor, which gave him ample time to write and left his mind free to compose. One of the more lucrative jobs he held during this period was piloting a helicopter to fly men and equipment to an offshore oil rig on the Gulf of Mexico, but he finally decided to quit this job because it didn't leave him enough time to write.

Kris' Rhodes Scholarship opened up numerous doors for him; he could have had any one of a multitude of high-paying, prestigious jobs, and today we might find his name mentioned in the pages of the *Wall Street Journal* as president of some conglomerate, or such. He chose, however, to bypass those doors and to pursue his earliest dream, that of becoming a songwriter. Even while struggling through the financially toughest times of his life, he passed up high-paying jobs offering security and prestige. Most notable of these was an offer to work at a very high level in a publishing company. Obviously it was not the money Kris was after. Even as a child, his parents had said that his brother Craig would be the money-maker of the family, but that Kris probably wouldn't make much money because he didn't care about it. It certainly seemed that way in those early Nashville days, but the irony of that remark is only too clear today, because Kris makes more money than anyone could have ever dreamed, and more than he ever cared to make.

When Kris first got to Nashville, he immediately sold one song: "Vietnam Blues." This song, an anti-protestor number, was in keeping with the Nashville mood of the times and rather unlike the rest of his work. But this song, too, was written from the heart. Kris had signed up for Vietnam duty, but instead had been assigned to the West Point teaching post. He wrote "Vietnam Blues" after witnessing several anti-Vietnam demonstrations, particularly one protest aimed at the family of an Army man who had been killed. Kris felt strongly that the protestors had no conception of the soldier's point of view. Although this song was well-received, Kris sold no others for the next several years.

It was a struggle just to stay alive during the years 1965 to 1969, and he alternated between wondering if he should stick it out or pack it in. But he held on. During those struggling times, it may have seemed as if things couldn't possibly get worse, but they did. His wife and he had separated twice, and finally she left him for good, taking their daughter, Tracy, and infant son, Kris, Jr. Their son had been born with a defective esophagus and Kris owed exorbitant hospital bills.

He took a ramshackle $25-a-month room in a rooming house and continued slaving over his songs. At this time he wrote "For the Good Times," reflecting on the good of his marriage and about the loss of love between two people. This song was particularly hard to sell, as it was considered too risqué for country music at the time. When Ray Price finally recorded it in 1970, it became a huge success and won 1970's "Song of the Year" award from the Country Music Association (CMA) over Merle Haggard's hard-line country hit "Okie from Muskogee." Ray Price also won a Grammy for his rendition of Kris' song. When it first appeared, however, many country radio stations refused to play it because it was too racy.

Eventually, Kris took a job at Columbia Studios cleaning ashtrays and carrying things around for $58-a-week. "The beauty of that one," he says, "was that I didn't have to think." It gave him more time to compose and to keep his mind open to songwriting. It also gave him the opportunity to get closer to people like Johnny Cash and to try and push his songs. Johnny Cash recalls that Kris seemed to be everywhere he was in those days. But that didn't seem to do him any good; his big break was a long way off.

Kris' family didn't approve, much less appreciate his life style or

Roy Clark   CMA Awards, 1970   *UPI*

ambitions. He constantly received letters from home with significant newspaper clippings about former classmates who had made it big in traditional ways. His parents wrote him one letter in which they told him that they just couldn't understand what made him tick. Later, though, they wrote to tell him that although they didn't condone or understand his choices, they were behind him. Today, his mother and sister Karen are the biggest country and western fans around. They call up radio stations and request his songs in disguised voices. (His father, unfortunately, didn't live to see his son's success.)

During those bleak years Kris, rejected by his wife and family, still held on, writing and working toward his goal. All the while he was soaking up

Nashville, and during this period he wrote some of his best and most successful songs including "Sunday Mornin' Comin' Down," which at the time, he couldn't sell to a soul. Times were so rough that several of his friends suggested that perhaps it was time to give up; but he was encouraged by those country stars with whom he had come in contact.

1976   *Frank Edwards/Fotos International*

Johnny Cash, in particular, was a source of encouragement. He had heard a tape of several of Kris' songs, which he liked very much, but which he says he felt too close to to record at the time. While Kris was still emptying ashtrays at Columbia studios, some friends nearly got him fired by trying to push his songs on Cash in the middle of a recording session. The next night,

26

Cash came down to the basement where Kris was working on some tapes and bummed a cigarette from him. He began telling him that he'd heard that Kris had gotten into some trouble recently. Kris felt like a fool. He explained that he'd had nothing to do with that disruption, and Cash said that he knew. He then invited Kris to come upstairs for the recording

Rita Coolidge   Radio City, NYC, 1977   *UPI*

session Cash was working on. When Kris objected, saying that he had been forbidden to go up there, Cash insisted, saying that he wouldn't hold the session without him. You can imagine Kris' feelings at that moment. It solidified his admiration for Cash, because he would take time out for a "nobody" like him.

UNICEF Show, 1979   *Chuck Pulin*

Kris remembers that evening as being a horrible experience. He sat on the floor of the studio, getting cold stares from all the musicians, all except Cash.

Cash had been noted for his interest in new writers and was one of the few musicians in Nashville to open his ears to the musical influences outside of country and include them in his repertoire. Cash's famous collaboration with Bob Dylan and his use of material from Gordon Lightfoot and others had established him as a man who was beginning to make a dent in the country music genre. While his work had been renowned and respected by the traditional country audience, he was paving the way for a wider country audience and broadening the horizons of the present one. It is no doubt that through Cash's influence, and a handful of others like him, that Kris' decidedly different country music was able to emerge when it did. Perhaps if Cash had not helped to open those doors, Kris would have had to wait even longer for his songs to gain acceptance.

Kristofferson had been compared to Cash in that both have the same rugged, untrained voices which make their renditions of songs unique, a quality which hints at rowdiness — a rough past, but through which can be felt a sensitive, intelligent individual. Like Cash, Kristofferson went through very rough times for years before making it. Today the two are best of friends, and although their schedules allow little time to see each other, they still remain close through letters and phone calls.

Another man who had begun to broaden the country music horizons was Roger Miller. Miller had heard a tape of Kris' songs and had liked what he'd heard. His future recording plans included at least one of Kris' songs: "Me & Bobby McGee." Finally in 1969, Roger Miller did record "Bobby McGee" as well as two others of Kris', including "Sunday Mornin' Comin' Down." "Bobby McGee" met with instant success, and Kris received a comfortable advance, which he used to pay bills.

The tide was beginning to turn, and Kris got a glimpse of the future. He was, by no means, at or even near the top, and the day was still a long way off when he could relax and feel comfortable and secure. In fact, Kris really doesn't rest on his laurels now — because when your job is to create, you can never be sure if what you will create tomorrow will be as popular as what you've created in the past. The funny thing about an audience is that it is unpredictable; the critics and the listeners are apt to change their minds and their preferences at any moment; popularity is a tenuous thing.

David Frost Show, 1973   *Chuck Pulin*

Radio City, NYC, 1977   *Chuck Pulin*

THE TURNING OF THE TIDE

Shortly before Kris' songs had become popular, and well before Kris himself was a familiar face in Nashville, he had been invited to a Nashville hotel room where Joni Mitchell had assembled a group of musicians for a jam session. There that night were Michael Nesmith, Graham Nash, and David Crosby as well as other musical friends. Throughout the evening, everyone offered up old and new songs, and the give and take of the session lasted until early in the morning. Finally, Joni turned to Kris, who had been silent the entire night, and asked him to play something. He was shy and mumbled something to the effect that he wasn't a singer. Finally, when everyone insisted, Kris pulled out a notebook from his pocket and said that he'd just read some of the new things he had been working on.

He did "Me & Bobby McGee" and "Sunday Mornin' Comin' Down" to the amazement of all listening. Afterwards, there was a full moment of silence as the beauty of Kris' lyrics sunk into everyone. Each person present knew that they had just heard something special.

The years 1969 and 1970 brought good fortune to Kris. Finally, after nearly five grueling years of doubt and despair, of hard work, and of losing virtually everything he had but his integrity, Kris was slowly beginning to find acceptance for his work.

Since Roger Miller's hit with "Bobby McGee," the song has been recorded by artists as diverse as Johnny Cash, the Grateful Dead, and Janis Joplin, who immortalized it. Her 1969 recording of "Me & Bobby McGee" became a million-plus seller, a number-one song for several weeks in the fall of '69, and a candidate for the best recording of the year. The popularity of that song also helped to bring her posthumous album *Pearl* to gold

31

The Troubador, LA, 1971   *Frank Edwards/Fotos International*

Taj Mahal, Big Sur, 1970   *Herbert Wise*

Ali McGraw Convoy *Hy Simon /United Artists*

record status. By 1972, "Me & Bobby McGee" had been recorded by more than fifty artists.

Looking back, it seems astounding that Kris had to peddle that particular song for so long. It is a country classic, and a prime example of the way in which Kris' best songs seem to have been with us since eternity, rather than having been written during our lifetimes. It talks of roaming, hitch-hiking, searching for a dream of freedom — what topics could be more country? What is more, the song tells a story, as do most classic country songs.

This song has all the right things going for it. The poetry is perfect, the lyrics have become catch-phrases that stand up admirably outside the

33

context of the song. "Freedom's just another word for nothin' left to lose" is certainly an oft-quoted line today. Kris is particularly proud of "feelin' near as faded as my jeans" because it is the kind of line that sounds as if you've heard it before. Another point of pride for Kris is the fact that it was probably the first time that New Orleans was rhymed with something other than

Madison Square Garden, NYC   *Chuck Pulin*

"Cajun Queens." It is the use of such unusual lines coupled with vibrant imagery that has marked Kris' writing, but it took Roger Miller to decide that country audiences were ready to handle the nature of the song.

"Me & Bobby McGee" gave listeners a first glimpse into the basic theme which can be traced throughout all of Kris' work. If there is one over-riding

Bee Gees, Billboard Awards   *Judi Lesta*

2074007

Madison Square Garden, NYC, 1973   *Chuck Pulin*

philosophical statement to be culled from his songs, it is that, for all of us, things have already been about as good as they can be expected to get. This is a general theme to be understood, not so much in day-to-day living, but as applied to society in general. In "Bobby McGee" it is fairly simple to extract this basic philosophy.

Miller's recordings were the first hint at the success Kris would soon achieve. During 1969 and 1970, the breaks started rolling in for him. Dennis Hopper (of *Easy Rider* fame) had heard a tape of Kris' songs, then entirely unknown and unrecorded. He offered Kris plane fare, expenses, and hotel accommodations if he wanted to write the score of his ill-fated, ironically titled *Last Movie*. Kris looks back at this as a major break. The filming was being done in Peru and Kris gladly accepted. At the time, he felt that the small sums of money he was getting for his work were fantastic. He believed that what he was getting then was about as good as it could be, and he was quite satisfied.

While in Peru, Kris received a telegram from Johnny Cash asking to use Kris' "Casey's Last Ride" on his TV show, and he asked him to join him on the show when he returned to Nashville. Cash has been Kris' staunchest supporter, pushing his songs and having him as a guest several times on his shows.

In 1969, Fred Foster, president of Monument Records, believing in Kris' talent, signed him to a recording contract. Kris was uncertain of his abilities as a performer, protesting "I sing like a goddam frog." But Foster convinced him that it was the best way to push his songs. He was soon to begin touring and recording under his own name and to become the legend that he is now in country music.

1970 was a special year for Kris. He met lots of new people and got a close-up of just how the music industry and its stars worked and lived. On June 23, the day after his thirty-third birthday, he made his club debut at The Troubador in Los Angeles as the opening act for Linda Ronstadt. He performed some of his songs which were later to become national best sellers for other singers, but for which he had yet to become known.

Melody Maker magazine said of this debut that Kris "proved to be one of the most exciting and unusual writer/performers around." The evening was especially exciting and, Kris received a very warm reception from the audience.

Rita, Candice Bergen, Willie Nelson, Burt Reynolds   Bottom Line, NYC, 1979   *Hy Simon*

As he was driving home from this, his first gig, he was stopped by a policeman who thought he had stopped him before. Kris had a bottle of "Binaca" breath freshener, and the policeman asked him what it was. Kris replied, "Oh, I shoot up Binaca." With that, the policeman smacked a pair of handcuffs on him, and he spent the night in jail. The next day, the cop came in to apologize saying that he'd realized who he was and that he'd recognized him from television.

Two months later, Kris made his New York club debut at the Bitter End and received rave reviews. Critics appreciated his shy stage personality and his new brand of country music. He was called a troubador, a folk singer,

Candice Bergen Bottom Line, NYC, 1979 *Hy Simon*

and a country writer. Despite attempts to categorize Kris, they loved what he brought to the stage.

After his big Troubador debut, Kris found himself to be something of a west coast celebrity and suddenly on numerous Hollywood guest lists. It was at this time that he landed his first role in a movie, thereby firmly implanting himself, in the same year, as both a new writer/performer as well as an actor.

This same year, Kris won the Country Music Association's award for "Song of the Year" for "Sunday Mornin' Comin' Down." Several years later, as a guest on the *Saturday Night Live* show, Kris explained his success with this particular song, characteristically, with his tongue in his cheek. "Like a lotta you, I had a handicap," he began. "I was a college graduate with degrees in literature and creative writing. And I couldn't get arrested! Then how did I write song that made me a legend in my own time? The answer's in this book: *Talk Country*. I got a chapter on nothin' but droppin' 'g's, an' another one on double negatives, and one on grammar that tells why nobody wanted a song called Sunday Morning Feeling Terribly Depressed or Bobby McGee and I."

Obviously, Kris understood only too well, the makings of salable, likable music, and was never too far removed from things to take a poke at himself.

1970 was a very good year for awards. The Academy of Country Music presented Kris with their "Song of the Year" award for "For the Good Times." and the Nashville Songwriters Association awarded Kris as "Songwriter of the Year!"

There it was — finally — acceptance, recognition, and acknowledgement. This was the beginning of his career as a bona fide songwriter, with the added plus of becoming a sought after performer, and budding actor. It marked the end of his struggling years.

Rod Stewart   UNICEF Show, 1979   *Chuck Pulin*

Rita Coolidge   Radio City, NYC, 1977   *Chuck Pulin*

HIS MUSIC

Although Kris' background, education and lifestyle distinguish him from other country performers and writers, his eloquent songs epitomize the finest in country music. Whether in spite of, or because of his differences from past country musicians, Kris Kristofferson's work stands among the most highly respected and widely performed music in the country genre.

Why then, was it so hard for Kris to find acceptance for his songs; to sell what are essentially traditional country lyrics and tunes to the Nashville market?

First of all, it should be remembered that when Kris entered the Nashville scene, country music was still very much southern oriented. Country music, right up to the seventies, was mired in its down-home roots, holding fast to tradition, refusing to give way to the social and political changes that had been ripping through the nation. Inherent in country music is its simple and sincere treatment of powerful emotions. Kris' work has gone even further in its emotional intensity and honesty. His contribution to Nashville, specifically, has been the theme of sexuality freely discussed and outwardly supported. Even in the mid-sixties, sexuality was not a topic which country writers cared to discuss openly.

It took men like Kristofferson to open the doors to a more cosmopolitan and sensitive country audience. "To many observers, Kristofferson seemed the embodiment of country music's liberation from its conservative, puritan, rural southern past," one critic noted. Kris' own involvement in the sixties, simply by virtue of his having lived through them, combined with his sensitive treatment of subjects formerly taboo in country music, have heralded the way for other songwriters in this genre. Willie

Billy Swan   Bottom Line, NYC, 1979   *Chuck Pulin*
Rod Stewart   UNICEF Show, 1979   *Chuck Pulin*

Buzzy Linhart, Madison Square Garden, NYC, 1973 *Chuck Pulin*

Nelson, Waylon Jennings, and Billy Joe Shaver are a few who have profited from Kris' advances.

Kris' songs, while dealing with typical country themes, are often couched in more urbane and intellectual moods than country music had been used to, and in dealing with these subjects, Kris' tone is often sarcastic. These interrelated reasons help to explain the resistance he met when his works were first heard.

If Kris made an impact on Nashville, it was in no small way because Nashville, in its own manner, was ready for him. Johnny Cash, a true country man, who had been to prison and back, had licked a drinking

Rod Stewart UNICEF Show, 1979 *Hy Simon*

David Frost Show, 1973   *Chuck Pulin*   UNICEF Show, 1979   *Chuck Pulin*

problem, and emerged as a gospel-spouting hero, was a popular performer who had been experimenting with new sounds. His approval was a great step forward. There was only so far that country music could progress without taking into account the changes that the rest of the music scene had already responded to. After all, what is music but a reflection of the various aspects of society? And Kris Kristofferson, though he worked hard to become accepted, has been influential in affecting this change in country music.

Rita Coolidge Radio City, NYC, 1977 *UPI*

He has been called a "leader of a new breed of folk/rock/country singers" and is greatly credited with helping to disintegrate the boundaries between these three styles of music. In the process, he has helped open up country music to a much wider audience. Country lyrics have always been more important than their melodies, and in Kris' work, this is also true. John Prine, one of Kris' "discoveries," says of Kris' early works that you need only to read the lyrics, and you will know the melody without hearing it.

There are two things that should be kept in mind about Kris Kristofferson,

Rita Coolidge Bottom Line, NYC, 1979 *Hy Simon*

one, that he is first and foremost a writer; he is a writer before he is a performer. The second is that his heart and his musical roots are in the country style. If he has helped to widen the scope of this music, it is because he is an intensely introspective man who needs to express his feelings and who has done so within a personal and original context. His style, though, can always be traced to country.

Kris is not anxious to analyze his works at any length. He feels that his lyrics are simple enough to be understood. Kris writes in a satirical manner; he takes simple notions and breaks them apart, uncovering inherent dualities. Much of what he says should not be taken at face value, it can be seen as poking fun at certain things — himself, and even at the country style. He uses the country style so effectively that his lyrics have often been taken as literally as possible.

There is a self-satirizing aspect of his work that has too often been mistaken for self-righteousness. His underlying theme, that this is by no means, the "best of all possible worlds," and that none such world exists — can be traced through all of his lyrics. From that premise, it should be understood that sarcasm is his mode of expression. This does not mean that he cannot write sincere songs. On the contrary, songs like "Bobby McGee" and "Sunday Mornin'" are the ultimate in honest songs because his theme is a lament, a realization, and an honest look through the veneer of society and self.

In this respect critics have been particularly insensitive to his expressions, at times, because they have looked at his work only on a one-dimensional level.

HIS ALBUMS, THE CRITICS

Kris' first album, originally entitled *Kristofferson* and later re-released as *Me & Bobby McGee*, appeared in the summer of 1970. Significantly, Johnny Cash wrote the liner notes for this debut album. This album, although one of his best, didn't show up on national charts until early September, 1971. His voice here is clear, sincere and shy. The songs have become, of course, legendary. He sings every word of his poems clearly because that is his main concern; he is the writer of these poems, and he is proud of them, wanting everyone to hear the words.

(Much later, Kris, lamenting the fact that his media image gets in the way of his true self, said that he no longer feels compelled to sing clearly and distinctly because he feels that people don't come to hear his poetry anymore, but to see an image.)

In a *Rolling Stone* review of the first album, Ray Rezos says that Kris "embodies the folksinger's tradition." He calls it a superb album and praises Kris' lyrics as "always right; he can be bitter, cynical when he has to be and then turn around and be poetically pretty without being saccharine."

What spurred this album's success was the release, in 1971, of *The Silver-Tongued Devil and I,* his second album. This album was widely accepted, and people began to appreciate not only his emotional, witty writing style, but his unusual voice. Neil Coppage, in *Stereo Review* magazine wrote that two of his ballads from this album, "Loving Her Was Easier," and "When I Loved Her" "illustrate particularly well how effectively he invents melodies that are perfect vehicles for his lyrics.

Without the words the melodies wouldn't be anything very special, but in context, they are extraordinary.''

The title track from *The Silver-Tongued Devil and I* is a barroom type of song, acoustic, with a true country-western flavor. Kris' rangy, barroom voice is especially effective in this song, which again, sounds not new, but instead, classic. Perhaps that is the one great thing about his work, that much of it sounds like classic C & W, which is certainly a compliment. In fact, if Kris once idolized Hank Williams, he has since been compared to him in that both men found that rare ability to pen bittersweet country classics.

This special mix of raucous acoustic songs, and haunting ballads brought *Silver-Tongued Devil* to gold record status in 1971. Many believe that Kris himself is the silver-tongued devil, and, indeed, it is an apt epithet.

In 1971, Kris' "Help Me Make it Through The Night," another classic, won numerous awards, including a Grammy for "Best Song of the Year," as well as a Grammy to Sammi Smith, whose version of this song brought her international popularity and won her "Best Female Vocalist." The Country Music Association voted her version as "Best Single of the Year," and for the second consecutive year, Kris won the Nashville Songwriters Association's "Songwriter of the Year" award.

After five years of struggling, he had become a respected country regular. In fact, by mid 1971, Kris had published approximately 130 songs.

By 1972 Kris was well into his movie career and had met Rita Coolidge, who became his constant companion and support and later his wife.

Kris released two solo albums in '72: *Border Lord* and *Jesus Was a Capricorn,* both of which made excellent use of Rita's rich, clear vocals.

The title song on *Border Lord* is a great analysis of a star's life on tour, as he straddles the boundary separating sanity from madness. Under the title on the album's cover, Kris wrote: " . . . Cruising pretty close to crazy, but somehow keeping it together enough to keep from crossing that border."

Kris' remarkable verbal abilities permeated this album, and songs of note from this LP include "Josie," "Stagger Mountain Tragedy," and "Somebody Nobody Knows."

Jesus Was a Capricorn reached gold status and was a hit from November of '72 through most of '73. On this album, a number of excellent songs are found. The title track clearly illustrates Kris' duality, and although this song is obviously a religious spoof, many took it seriously. "Jesse Younger" is a

Murray the K, Imus, Richie Havens, Rita, Kris, Denise Nichols,   *Chuck Pulin*
Bill Withers, Buzzy Linhart, Mary Travers Madison Square Garden, NYC

Bottom Line, NYC, 1979   *Chuck Pulin*

song with a real mountain flavor, full of those rich C & W sounds and intonations, yet with a rather urbane twist. It is the story of a boy who disappointed his parents by going his own way, regardless of their values. He is not actually a hero in this song, because the tone is rather sullen. This

Grammy Awards, Hollywood, 1974 *Frank Edwards/Fotos International*

song can be taken either in modern ties or seen as an old tune in an old-time setting.

"Why Me Lord," another religious spoof, which, however, was seen by a tremendous amount of fans as serious, drips of an extra sing-songy tune and uses just the right touches of sarcasm and authenticity aided by Rita's airy gospel sounds in the background. This song was a big hit during 1973.

Perhaps the most powerful song on this album is "Sugar Man." It is an extremely melodramatic, New Orleans sounding tune, not at all stylized, almost bluesy. The song is a whorehouse lullabye, sung with just the right tone of resignation in the rangy way that only Kris could evoke.

"Nobody Wins," a true C & W classic sounding tune, with appropriate lyrics, recalls the Hank Williams style for which Kris is alone in his ability to elicit.

Critics compared these two albums unfavorably with Kris' first two outstanding albums. A number of critics complained that Kris' acting career was getting in the way of his writing, that his albums seemed like afterthoughts, and that his songs lacked the polish of his former songs. They said that they didn't ring as true as his past efforts, that in fact, they seemed like efforts rather than inspired moments. One criticism was that Kris was no longer a man "with an empty belly" and that, therefore, he was unable to write as he had before. The validity of a statement like that is negated by its subjectivity. The question of physical hunger being a catalyst for creativity can be argued till the end of time. If a person is a true artist, then his own mind will remain hungry for new ideas and expressions, and we know that Kris never looked on his writing as a means to solve financial problems. His lyric abilities are always apparent throughout his songs, perhaps not always at the same standard of excellence, but certainly he had not dried out as a lyricist by 1972.

Bill Anderson, an extremely successful country songwriter, said about Kris: "He has written about a half-dozen perfect songs, and that, believe me, is a lot."

During 1972 and 1973, Kris was involved in movies, and both he and Rita toured together constantly. This new dimension to his performances was at first welcomed. Their concerts received overwhelmingly laudatory reviews for the sincerity and warmth which emanated from the two as they performed touching duets of Kris' most popular works. The combination of Kris' rough baritone and Rita's luxurious, soulful voice was applauded in a series of sold-out concerts.

Kris once praised Rita's singing in this eloquent way: "She can take a piece of crap I wrote and make it sound incredible." This is probably true, as her origins in choir singing and her natural talent can transform any piece of music into a meaningful number. Prior to joining Kris, she had been a sought after back-up vocalist (and pianist) for the likes of Eric Clapton, Graham Nash, and Boz Scaggs, and had been an important factor in Joe Cocker's and Leon Russell's highly successful *Mad Dogs & Englishmen* tour. In fact, Leon Russell's popular song "Delta Lady" was written as a tribute to Rita.

At the time that she met Kris, however, she was in the beginning stages of striking out on her own and has since recorded a number of successful solo albums. She was tired of the superstar life and the "Delta Lady" tag and had always wanted to work with a ballad. With Kris, she got the opportunity.

In 1973, Kris and Rita received a Grammy for "Best Group Performance" for "From the Bottle to the Bottom," while Kris again, for the third time, received the Nashville Songwriters Association's award for "Songwriter of the Year."

That summer, Kris and Rita were regular cast members of the NBC summer replacement show *Country Music*. Kris and Rita went on to record a number of albums together beginning with *Full Moon* on A & M and their aptly titled *Breakaway*, which appeared in 1974. *Breakaway* is a collection of songs, some up tempo and some ballads written by Kris, Larry Gatlin, and Donnie Fritts, among others. Under the title on the album's back, Kris wrote the credits to the musicians and followed it with this: "They are generous gentlemen and blessed with the incredible talents of Rita Coolidge." Kris' esteem for Rita's abilities is a tribute to her.

The song "Slow Down" on this album, written by Kris, seems to summarize his general mood at the time; it might have been the album's theme song, or his and Rita's theme song at the time, as it seems to parallel the title. For example, the lyrics repeat this maxim over and again, "Slow down and try to do the thing that's right for you."

Also of note on this album is the song "I've Got to Have You," which has been recorded by many other artists. It is a beautiful love song with a haunting refrain. What makes this album so likable is the old-fashioned way the two trade off verses of each song, just like an old front porch kind of family sing-along.

Radio City, NYC, 1977 *Chuck Pulin*

Bottom Line, NYC, 1979 *Chuck Pulin*

During a 1974 concert in Cumming, Georgia, Kris found himself attacked, rather than by a screaming female fan, as happens to so many stars, but by a crusty older man. A problem with the sound system caused a great deal of annoyance for the performers, and Kris vocalized his complaints loudly and angrily. When he cooled down, he promptly apologized for his behavior. "I'm sorry," he told the audience. "I'm just (*expletive deleted.*)" This incensed an angry member of the audience who shouted "What did you say?" Before Kris could respond, the man ran up to the stage, grabbed Kris by the hair, and began to drag him off!!

In an equally bizarre incident the following year, a man in Albuquerque, New Mexico, filed a $2,000,000 lawsuit against Kris and Combine Music Corp. for having stolen a song that he claimed to have written, "Help Me Make it Through The Night." James I. Morgan said that Kris obtained the copyright without securing his permission and that both Kris and Combine "obtained copyright for the purpose of misleading the public as to who wrote the song."

Kris' *Spooky Lady's Sideshow* appeared in 1974, the same year as *Breakaway*. In a *Rolling Stone* review, Stephen Holden hailed *Spooky Lady* as perhaps the best of Kris' career and noted that it was the first produced outside of Nashville. In a few words, Holden captured the essence of Kris' lyrics. "While on one level his songs tell of personal and social alienation, they also carry a strain of irony, his most down-and-out laments suggesting in their lyric indulgence and vocal intonation deliberate self-parody, a sense of the absurd."

This is the essence of Kris' writing. In *Spooky Lady's Sideshow*, some classic examples of the brilliance of Kris' lyric sense can be found. The songs range from those of lost love and broken dreams, and one that he calls "whimsically ironic" (Kris' usual assortment) to one fabulous epic entitled "Rescue Mission," which brings out Kris' literary talents as distinguished from simple songs. It's a wonder that this song didn't receive more attention. It has the sound and rhythm of a Coleridge poem, and it reads equally as exciting as a poem, as it sounds enthralling as a song.

"Rescue Mission" was written with the help of Roger McGuinn, Bobby Neuwirth and Seymore Cassell. It tells a story of a battle taking place on a schooner, setting a full scene where each character comes alive. It is vivid! It takes place toward the end of the battle in which the sailors are losing badly, and is sung by Kris and Bobby Neuwirth who trade off verses until the last one in which each does two lines, jumping in on the end of the last. This song surely ranks among the very best of Kris' work.

Other songs of note on *Spooky Lady's Sideshow* are "Same Old Song," in which Kris writes about the climb toward success and remarks that "the bottom ain't so different from the top, just a few more friends you'll be losin' when you drop." Could he have coined yet another phrase? And is he alluding to the fact that he is well aware that a drop can come about much easier than a rise?

The refrain of this song explains something on which critics have been harping, the idea that a success cannot write songs of sadness. " . . . And the sweet just a little bit sweeter/But them blues, well it's just the same old song."

"Shandy (The Perfect Disguise)" is also a very good song, as it once again illustrates Kris' depth and ability to create phrases which use words in sequences that bring forth new meanings.

"Broken Freedom Song" is an interesting look at the ways in which personal freedom can be loneliness. It is three vignettes of lonely, lost people, followed by a chorus echoing that loneliness.

Apart from the excellent lyrics which *Spooky Lady* contains, the back cover is priceless. Kris has written spoof reviews, all bad, of his work and assigned fictitious names and magazines to them, which are quite telling. Finally, he has gotten his feelings across about the critics. It asserts his feelings that no matter how many records you sell, bad reviews still go to the heart. For example, one review reads: "Ambitious — if woefully inept — attempt to GO DEEP, complete with silly Dylan-Dali image imitations and what looks dangerously like A CONCEPT behind the whole thing. A new low in the artist's often competent, but steadily settling career. SURREALLY, Kris!"
Bascombe Yves St. John—*ROLLING STONED*

Another review also gets to the crux of the problem as seen by Kris: "If one looks closely enough, the temptation to link particular songs to particular ladies in the singer's crowded past is irresistible. And there are clues a-plenty!"
Ed Limesucker—*SHOWBIZ SNOOPER*

Kris finally did get his jab at the critics, but, even this superb album was

Rita Coolidge Bottom Line, NYC, 1979 *Hy Simon*

not well received and no one seemèd to mention his remarks on the back. Critic Hilburn, who Kris feels made his career in his early years, panned *Spooky Lady*, saying that Kris' lyrics were repetitious. The suggestion, on the part of Hilburn as well as others, was that now that Kris had really made it to stardom, with all its trappings, he was no longer the lonely, disgruntled freedom seeker he once was when he penned some of the classic songs of our age. Can this be a case where the shoe is on the other foot? That now that Kris *has* made it to the top, that critics cannot get that out of their minds, and therefore refuse to view the man aside from his image as they have created it? Well, he has answered this attack in his songs. Of course, a case can be made that loneliness, melancholia, etc. breed good poetry in the creative mind, and when things go well there is simply no poetry; happiness breeds sappiness. However, this is not the case with Kris, because as has been noticed all throughout his life, Kris' poetry doesn't necessarily revolve around the physical aspects of his life, but the spiritual and philosophical tenets in which he believes. His poetry springs from an inner dissatisfaction or happiness, and only secondarily from the outer aspects of his life. And, of course, critics are individuals with preferences which color their reviews; while one may praise a work, another may claim it to be the worst piece of junk ever written.

Aside from personal preferences, Kris feels that his media image, from movies, and especially as created by writers themselves, influences their understanding of his lyrics. Where once they were willing to see the sarcasm in his tunes, now they see only the superficial side. We are a hyper-critical society and too often turn aside from those we embrace once they are no longer underdogs. "As soon as you get to a certain point, it's no longer hip to dig you," Kris remarked, pointing to the situation where critics had panned the Eagles for the same things they had praised them for before. It's a perverse society that makes stars from nobodies and soon afterward relishes in their destruction. If you look at the course of Kris' career, you can see him pushing songs for years, which, when finally accepted, received accolades as the greatest thing since Hank Williams, and consequently catapulted Kris to stardom. These songs, a few years before untouchable, made him the poet of his generation, and then he is criticized for carrying on the very tradition he started. "It gets to the point where a writer can't write a song without having to ask himself 'Why did I write this?'" Kris complained. When a song simply springs from his mind, as an inspiration, a fragment, or a full-blown idea, he hones the song/poem, going over each segment until he has a feeling for it, until he understands it. Once the song's finished, that's it; as he puts it, "the umbilical cord's cut."

Naturally, he is open to criticism, but it's certainly disconcerting to find yourself nothing one day, a king the next, and to know that you can continue bobbing back and forth between the two extremes as long as you're in the public eye. Of course, that's a star's problem once he chooses to become visible. "We're all a little unstable," Kris said, "or else we wouldn't be up on stages making fools of ourselves."

Billy Swan Bottom Line, NYC, 1979 *Hy Simon*

Movies had begun to take up an increasing amount of Kris' time, but he still managed to satisfy his fans and to release an album per year. 1975's offering was *Who's to Bless and Who's to Blame*, which featured both Kris and Rita in the spotlight. Again, Rita's beautiful interpretation blends nicely with Kris' voice, which by this time had picked up a few singing tricks from Rita.

The following year, Kris released his album *Surreal Thing*, a title which seems to be a pun on the catch-phrase of the time, "It's the real thing." With Kris' humor in mind, it can be taken as a mocking statement about our manufactured reality.

Songs of Kristofferson, a "best-of" album, followed and serves as a good summary of this legendary writer's best material, but as it is only one album, so many good songs had to be left out from the collection.

Easter Island is Kris' latest solo album and features ten new songs all written or co-written by Kristofferson and well-known musicians Stephen Bruton and Mike Utley. Once again, Rita and Billy Swan aid Kris in his presentation. These people are the core of musicians with whom Kris has collaborated over the years, and they work well together, evoking the sounds for which Kris has become famous. Each of these individuals has gone on to do work of their own, and has found personal success in the music industry.

Natural Act is Kris' latest album. It is a duo effort shared with Rita and features a variety of old and new tunes. After being on the market only a few weeks, the LP has made a great success; some major record stores report that they have sold out all of their copies.

Kris and Rita's recent tour promoting the new album brought them to the Bottom Line in New York, an intimate cafe, where they performed to sold-out houses for three consecutive nights.

HIS MOVIES

After Kris' triumphant debut at the Troubador, he found himself to be something of a celebrity and was invited to a number of Hollywood parties. One night at a party at Jack Nicholson's house, Fred Roos, who had been the casting director for *Five Easy Pieces* asked Kris if he'd like to audition for a part in an upcoming movie called *Two Lane Blacktop*. Kris said sure and was told to show up at Columbia Studios the following day. Although he had never done a movie before, nor had he acted, he felt that so long as he could read the script, get a feeling for the story, and gain a rapport for the character he was to play, then he could act. Several friends suggested that he take professional acting lessons before getting into movies, but he felt that he would try it his way.

His reason for being interested in movies was because he felt it might be a good idea to leave the music business behind for a while. Since he was having success with other performers recording his songs, his initial goals were being met. Kris is, after all, a songwriter before he is a performer. He had recently spent some time with Janis Joplin and had seen what the music business had done to her, how it had eaten her up. Only a short time later, he had learned of her death. Kris had begun to wonder if the musician's life was at all compatible with happiness or sanity.

Reflecting on Janis' death, a few years later Kris said, "You devote your whole life to entertaining people who, in the end, depress you so much you off yourself; that's a killer outfit." Kris doesn't like discussing the Joplin story; he feels that all of it is exploiting her.

Kris showed up at Columbia Studios that next morning, still a bit hung over from the previous night's party, not quite sure if he was meant to go to the Columbia Recording studio or the Columbia Picture studio. When he found out *Two Lane Blacktop* was a movie about cars, he simply said, "Can't even change a tire," and walked out.

He didn't get the part in that movie, but he was offered a part in *Cisco Pike*, which he accepted. The movie is about a formerly successful rock musician who gets coerced by a former policeman into running a marijuana deal, the proceeds of which will supplement the ex-cop's pension. It's sort of a dead-end story about Cisco's attempts to get back into music and his misadventures with this dope deal. Kris liked the script, felt he could identify with the character, Cisco, and he took the part. Karen Black starred as Cisco's girlfriend and Gene Hackman (who else?) played the crazed ex-cop.

While the movie was not a smash hit, it did get good reviews and served to introduce Kris as a bona fide movie actor. *Newsweek* magazine praised the movie as important for introducing a "talented young actor who has already established himself as the most interesting of the new Nashville folk-rock balladeers." Kris, himself, was fairly pleased with his first jab at acting, although he felt the ending of the movie was a little contrived, a sort of nowhere ending.

Kris feels that the movie was significant for him, because it led him to his role as Billy the Kid in Sam Peckinpah's celebrated *Pat Garret and Billy the Kid* in 1972.

Working with Peckinpah was something that Kris was looking forward to, and later said that he would like to always work with directors of this stature and vibrance. Unfortunately, this movie was not one of Peckinpah's better endeavors. In fact, it was generally panned as inept, boring, and poorly made. Kris' role as Billy did, however, receive good reviews, and so his movie career continued in good standing.

The movie received a great deal of attention mainly because it featured Bob Dylan in his first motion picture role. He played Alias, Billy's mysterious sidekick, although, unfortunately, his performance was not convincing. Dylan wrote the music for this movie, which was considerably more in his line of work, and several of the tunes from the score became huge hits, most notably "Knockin' on Heaven's Door."

Kris was instrumental in bringing Dylan into the movie, and this is a fact of which Kris is not all that proud. It seems that Dylan wasn't anxious to be

Barbra Streisand A Star Is Born   *Frank Edwards/Fotos International*

Ali McGraw Convoy   *Hy Simon/United Artists*

captured permanently on the screen, although he was interested in learning about making movies. Kris persuaded him that there could certainly be no better way to learn about movies than being involved in one and getting paid to learn at the same time. He told Dylan that the only reason he, himself, got into movies was to learn about acting. So, Dylan brought his

Convoy *Hy Simon/United Artists*

entire family to the town of Durango, Mexico, where the movie was being filmed. Reporters by the score were attracted to the movie set, and a tremendous amount of attention was paid to Dylan's presence. Dylan, as is characteristic, shunned reporters, remaining shy and reticent, and grew more and more edgy about the whole venture. His scenes in the movie were few and awkward and even though Kris helped to rewrite most of Dylan's scenes, his character, Alias, remained undeveloped. Kris' main objection to Dylan's role is that the two never seem to relate as characters, and in fact, that is one of the critics main objections to the movie as a whole.

Rita Coolidge played a minor role as Kris' woman, (even more minor,

Barbra Streisand and Jon Peters 1976 *UPI*

reports one paper, after she refused to do a nude scene). During the filming, as she was walking onto the set, she hit her head on a clay jug hanging from a tree. One observer said that when the foreign critics saw the movie, they'd be sure to note that only Peckinpah could make Rita look so starry-eyed at the first sight of Billy.

A Star Is Born   *Hy Simon/Warner Bros.*

Pat Garrett and Billy the Kid   *UPI*

During a break in the filming, Kris and Rita left to give a concert at Philharmonic Hall in New York. Rita's appearance was a welcome surprise and Kris also pleased the audience by bringing out a few talented friends, Willy Nelson and the legendary Al Kooper. The audience was genuinely moved by Kris' and Rita's tender duo of "Help Me Make It Through The Night."

The following year, Kris made *Blume in Love* with George Segal, Susan Anspach, and Marsha Mason and directed by Paul Mazursky of *Bob and Carol and Ted and Alice* fame. Mazursky wrote and directed this film which essentially deals with the same theme as *B & C & T & A*. *Blume* is the story of a successful young Los Angeles divorce lawyer, Blume (played by Segal) who for some unknown reason takes his secretary home to bed one afternoon and is discovered by his wife (Susan Anspach) who immediately, upon seeing this, wants a divorce. The movie becomes the story of Blume's attempts to win her back. In the process, '60s "involvement," modern marriage, and hypocrisy are the major topics brought out.

71

Barbra Streisand and Jon Peters A Star Is Born *Frank Edwards/Fotos International*

Barbra Streisand and Jon Peters A Star Is Born *Frank Edwards/Fotos International*

A Star is Born *Hy Simon/Warner Bros.*

Frank Edwards/Fotos International

Kris plays the part of Elmo, a fairly stereotyped "hippie" who is (you guessed it) a chronically unemployed musician, who has lived from town to town on welfare, sleeping in his van, playing guitar, and constantly getting high. He meets Blume's ex-wife at the welfare office where she works. She asks him how he can exist the way he does. He replies, "Nothin' to it," which is his attitude about life and a line he uses over and over throughout the movie. Elmo is a good-natured, lovable character, a classic free-spirit type. In the movie, Kris' character brought out Gable-like characteristics, which writer Tom Burke described as a "strong, old fashioned blend of sexuality and niceness." Gable was so revered, Burke suggests, because his "sexuality was good humored; it didn't challenge other males" while it did attract females. This is an apt description of Kris' appeal. It endears both sexes to him. He is both a hero-type and a lover-type.

In general, this movie was seen as funny, but some felt that what Mazursky thought was cutting satiric comedy, was in fact, baseless over-worked satire without substance. As seemed to be the case with many movies in which Kris starred, his acting was picked from among the rubble and praised. Vincent Canby, writing for *The New York Times*, said "Kristofferson, so ill at ease in Peckinpah's *Pat Garrett & Billy the Kid*, is most relaxed and debonnaire as the musician." *Time* magazine wrote, "Kris' Elmo is relaxed and appealing. Besides a great deal of what seems like effortless ability, Kristofferson has vast charm and the sort of presence that makes you look forward to his every appearance. He is, naturally and winningly, what so many others strain so hard to be: a star." The consensus was that Kris' charm emanates from within and embodies his performances.

Blume in Love opened at the Cannes Film Festival which Kris attended with Rita. It was the first time that many of the movie people had the opportunity to meet Rita, and since neither had ever been to the Riviera before, they gladly accepted the offer to go there for free.

While there, they even attended a few "movie star parties," but they are not much the type for that sort of gathering and the people who attend them. Rita's own recollection of a Hollywood party she had once been to sums up the way both Kris and Rita feel about these affairs. She was standing around talking to a few people, when someone accidentally knocked her elbow, and she spilled her glass of wine on the front of her dress. Everyone FROZE, she remembers. She turned around to get something with which to wipe it off, and when she turned back again, they had all left — disappeared! "That, to me," Rita says, "is a Hollywood party."

Just before leaving Cannes, although late for his plane, Kris took the time to return a car that had been provided for him by the Warner Bros. publicist. He dropped the car off at the man's hotel and left a thank-you note on the front seat. The publicist was shocked. "A movie star did that," he said. Kris' reaction, "You mean in movies, nobody *ever* says thanks for anything?"

A spate of movies followed, and Kris generally did well, but got parts which only hinted at his acting abilities. He invariably played a nice guy in roles which didn't allow for him to develop as an actor. One exception to the nice guy typecasting was a very small part Kris played in another poor Peckinpah movie, *Bring Me the Head of Alfredo Garcia.* Kris played Paco, a member of a motorcycle gang who happens into the scene and rapes the lead character's woman, only to get killed by him.

Kris' next major movie was *Alice Doesn't Live Here Anymore* directed by Martin Scorsese, known for *Mean Streets.* Kris played the sincere farmer who wins the heroine Alice's heart (played by Ellen Burstyn) because of his honesty and patience. This movie received a lot of attention as a film which presented women in a "new" light. Coming out, as it did, in the midst of the Women's Movement's heyday, it was thought to be a first in showing women solving their own problems, rather than as seen in the old Hollywood way. Many reviewers, however, didn't see it as pulling off this view effectively, in fact some claimed that Alice herself simply drifts by on a dream which, unfortunately, is based on something other than reality.

Kris' part in the movie was interpreted by some as the embodiment of the old Hollywood characterization of a woman's role transferred to a male. His character was willing to give up all to follow Alice as she attempted to play out her fantasy of becoming a singer. Unfortunately, she had a terrible voice. Kris played a man who had worked very hard to earn his farm, which afforded him a rich, full life, which he gives up to follow Alice.

Again, Kris received good reviews for his portrayal of a once again, lovable character. The *Village Voice* called him the most appealing leading man since Charles Boyer, and Judith Crist said that he was, "as always, more interesting than his roles seemingly allow." *Variety* summed up the

A Star Is Born *Hy Simon/Warner Bros.*

majority opinion of the critics in its review. "Kristofferson still manages to overcome a lot of his roles, projecting a worldly wise warmth that hopefully a fine script and director will bring out fully one day soon."

Whatever the case, his character is again Gable-like, as he plays the good-natured romantic. Rex Reed said that, in this movie, Kris did the best work of his acting career. It might seem as if he is being typecast into Gable sort of roles, but he certainly possesses all the characteristics to fit the bill. As his work shows, he seems most at east in this sort of role, although he doesn't wish to pursue a single type of character. It just seems that he is believable as an easy-going guy with a big heart and the promise of the good life.

The Sailor Who Fell from Grace with the Sea was a movie which Kris really enjoyed making. He composed its haunting musical theme, called

"The Sailor." He studied the part of the sailor intensely, living the part as a child would. He felt he knew the character, the story, and the setting inside out. But when he saw the movie, he was extremely disappointed with his performance. He said that he realized how far he had to go as an actor. The movie was adapted from a best selling novel written by the Japanese author of renown, Yukio Mishima, who was three times nominated for the Nobel Prize in literature, and heralded by the *NYT Book Review* as "a master of gorgeous and perverse surprises." The story is a chilling and touching tale of an American merchant seaman (Kris) who falls in love with a young widow (Sara Miles). She offers him a release from his disenchantment with the sea, and in her love for him, she finds a release for the sensuality she has repressed since her husband's death. Her thirteen-year-old son, who has a deep attachment to the sea and sailing, is a member of a teenage conspiracy of boys headed by a "dangerously precocious" bully known as "the chief." At first, Jonathan (the son) and his friends view the sailor as the ultimate masculine being, but when they learn that the sailor is giving up the sea to marry Jonathan's mother, the boys' disappointment is twisted by the bully to be another sign of "adult betrayal." The son and his friends then plan the sailor's destruction, because he has violated their beliefs in manhood. It is easy to see why Kris was so anxious to be in this movie as it is a graceful and chilling story.

While he does seem to play an interesting character, his own assessment of his acting in this movie is close to the truth. His acting does come off a little stiff, and it seems that he is tense in the part. But the strange story is compelling. Overall, he was believable, but his acting was not up to par. Perhaps the main repercussion of this movie was a weird sideline involving *Playboy* magazine, Kris, and Sara Miles. Apparently, Sara Miles had agreed with *Playboy* to do studio pictures of some of the more torrid scenes from the movie. Although Sara had agreed, Kris was undecided as to whether or not he would do these scenes at all despite assurances that he could approve whatever was to be printed. One night, it seems he was loaded, and it was rather late, and Sara Miles called him about it. He decided why not go ahead and do it. That, obviously was a mistake, as the pictures he says he approved were not those which were printed, and the whole affair caused a scandal. You can imagine Rita's feelings at seeing this! Her friends were constantly calling her about it. She was continually reminded of it

Convoy   *Hy Simon/United Artists*

Ernest Borgnine and Franklyn Ajaye   Convoy   *Hy Simon/United Artists*

which only served to aggravate her anger and hurt pride. She has said that she intends to be married only once, and that she had waited as long as she did because she wanted to be sure of her decision. This *Playboy* affair almost ended the marriage. She left Kris taking their daughter Casey with her. She realized, though, that their love was strong enough to overcome the crazy incident and, although her pride and faith were shaken, she did return home to the man she loves and who sincerely loves her.

Kris has said of this incident that it was just about the worst thing that he'd ever done. He realizes just how much he hurt Rita, and was told by many friends that he disgraced himself and his profession. All he can say of the matter is that he doesn't know why he did it. Luckily, it is now in the past, and Kris' and Rita's life has happily continued.

The photos were the most explicit ever involving major stars and were both praised and damned in trade circles. The film itself was rated R yet does not contain the graphic scenes which were published in the magazine.

After seeing *Sailor* and being as disappointed as he was with his acting, Kris said that he wondered if he should take time off for acting lessons. At the time, however, he was looking forward to his next movie and didn't have the time.

The movie which Kris looked forward to making, and which certainly received a great deal of press, was *A Star Is Born*. Much was written about the making of this movie, probably more controversy surrounded this film than any other with which Kris was involved. Certainly *Pat Garrett and Billy the Kid* received a lot of attention from the media, mainly because of Dylan's association with it, and as far as *Star* is concerned, most of the publicity, (most of it bad) centered around Barbra Streisand's volatile personality.

The movie was to be a remake of the popular original and even more popular second version which starred Judy Garland and James Mason. The new twist would be that the characters were contemporary rock figures, and the theme would revolve around the difficulties of today's rock world. It has been said that Kris decided to do this picture because he was under the impression that he could showcase his band in it and that he thought it would be a lucid picture, a "true statement" of the pressures of the music business. Kris himself said that he felt he could identify with the part, and could empathize with the character of a near washed-up musician. After all,

Ali McGraw Convoy   *Hy Simon /United Artists*

Convoy   *Hy Simon /United Artists*

his criterion for doing pictures was, along with a feeling for the entire story, an empathy for the character he will play.

Kris does not extract the role he plays for the story: he views it as a whole, and you will remember that was one of his criticisms of *Pat Garrett*, that the characters never were expanded enough to relate. Kris felt about *Star* that if he couldn't play a self-destructive musician, then what could he play? "I play that every day."

During the making of the movie, Kris threatened to quit numerous times. His major complaints were that Barbra and her entourage, her boyfriend-producer Jon Peters in particular, took total control of every aspect of the movie. Kris had not even been asked to write a song for it, no less asked to approve or venture an opinion of the music for the movie. A case can be made that both Kris' and Barbra's explosive personalities eventually led to more dynamic performances between the two. At least, Kris seems to feel that, after all is said and done, the tension, though much of it unnecessary, was a plus. Kris is the kind of guy who can look back, with a smile, and view it as a good experience. He even says he likes Barbra.

As far as the movie itself is concerned, there is no doubt that Barbra dominated the screen, that her character was more developed than Kris'. Even though Norman (Kris) committed a noble act in the picture for Esther's (Barbra's) career, and we knew and expected it, this crucial part was barely understandable in terms of Norman's character. We saw only the act and its effects.

As far as the sound track album goes, it was pretty much a fiasco. Many rock critics didn't care for Paul Williams' score, and *Rolling Stone* called it "the worst kind of histrionic supper-club stuff." Kris sings only three songs on the album, sounding awkward, as if he doesn't belong there, and Barbra's voice is mixed way out in front. One reviewer said that Kris' awkwardness on the album endeared Kris to him. The one song that did make a hit with twelve-year-olds and sixty-year-olds alike, "Evergreen" was written by Paul Williams and sung by Barbra. Despite all the criticism, Kris won a Golden Globe Award in 1977 as "Best Actor" for his performance in that movie.

Perhaps the most important aspect of *Star* was that it made Kris take a dramatic look at his life and change himself. While Rita says that Kris was definitely NOT playing himself in the movie, still, he saw certain aspects of

Ali McGraw   Convoy   *UPI*

himself which were exaggerated in the character he played and they suddenly seemed gross. He was so repulsed that he did something about them.

The first and major thing was his drinking. It was surely destroying him, but it was a part of him. He was truly an alcoholic, drinking tequila, among other things, by the bottle. It was just a part of the way he functioned. Asked how he could have produced all the great songs and done all the concerts and movies while drinking at the incredible pace he did, he simply replied that he could not have done it without it. *Star* made him see that kind of character in such an ugly light that he finally gave up drinking and hasn't drunk since. He now claims that it changed his whole life. He feels fresher, more alive now.

Convoy *UPI*

The other very important aspect of *Star* is that it made him think about how he would deal with Rita's success. The timing was fortuitous because now her albums are outselling his. Luckily for both, they are able to handle Rita's status as a superstar and have been able to put aside all jealousies which could have arisen as she gained the limelight. Both enjoy seeing the other's success. This can be a difficult problem in any marriage, and in the high-key life of the show business industry, it is even more difficult.

Semi-Tough, the first of Kris's two most recent movies, is a story of football, sensitivity training, and general antics. It was adapted from the successful book of the same name written by Dan Jenkins, a *Sports Illustrated* senior writer. David Merrick bought the book and originally planned to do it as a Broadway musical. Luckily, after hearing a few of the proposed songs, that idea was scrapped, and the movie got underway. Michael Ritchie, of *Bad News Bears* fame was the director. He says, ''My movie is a serious tribute to frivolousness.''

It is a satirical comedy about a rowdy football team and two star players, in particular, played by Burt Reynolds and Kris, both of whom had played college football and insisted on running their own plays in the movie. The men who were hired to act as members of the opposing teams, many of whom were actual pro-footballers and college athletes, were afraid at first to ''hit'' either of the two stars. But soon enough, Kris and Burt were getting hit like the rest of them. Somehow, the film goes into an EST-like adventure and actually makes a fair statement about the whole ''self-help'' movement which has been plaguing the '70s. In all, it is a funny, satiric look at a few things, two of them being football and this ridiculous craze. Jill Clayburgh plays the woman in the movie and is delightful as she curses with the best of them in her own charming manner.

Kris won raves for his role in this box-office hit.

Kris' latest movie is *Convoy* produced by Robert M. Sherman, directed by Sam Peckinpah, and filmed entirely on location around Albuquerque and Santa Fe, New Mexico. The screenplay for this movie is based on C. W. McCall's hit song of the same name, latching onto the tremendously popular topic of truckers and C. B. radios. In this film, Kris plays ''Rubber Duck,'' the leader of a group of truckers who form a giant convoy of their massive trucks and roar across the nation ''seeking justice from the harrassment of petty officialdom.'' Also starring in this film are Ali MacGraw, Ernest Borgnine, Burt Young, Madge Sinclair, and Franklyn Ajaye.

TODAY & FUTURE, KRIS & RITA

With movies, recording, and touring, these days Kris and Rita find the best way to relax from their hectic schedules is to be in the confines of their own home. They live with their daughter Casey in a fantastic ranch house in Malibu Hills, California, on acres of land. The house gives them the comfort and cozy feelings that make it home.

"The family unit is a base," says Kris, "contact with reality that you can come back to, which gets increasingly important to me. I care more about hanging out with my kids than I do about boogie-ing anymore."

Kris is still friendly with his first wife, who lives near his family in California, and their two children, Tracy and Kris, Jr., spend a part of their time with Kris and Rita, even accompanying them on tour occasionally. Kris says that the lesson he wants to impart to his children is that they should always think and grow. He says he wants to raise his kids with a great deal of freedom so they can "develop as their imaginations allow." If there is anything he doesn't want to do it is to "limit their ambitions." He wants to encourage them to grow rather than to "settle."

It seems as if his own experiences in seeking out the roads which were right for him, rather than following the prescribed paths, taught him a valuable lesson. If he were to restrict the comings and goings of his children or to try to channel their interests, he would be producing them, instead of allowing them to chart their own lives.

In retrospect, Kris has said that he would not like to re-live his life, but he feels everything about it, including all ups and downs, is a part of what he is today.

Kris and Rita have good relationships with both their families. It is especially important for Kris, now, to have all the family trouble behind him,

UNICEF Show, 1979   *Chuck Pulin*

Bottom Line, NYC, 1979   *Chuck Pulin*

Rita Coolidge UNICEF Show, 1979   *Chuck Pulin*

Rita Coolidge   David Frost Show, 1973   *Chuck Pulin*

as it is one more aspect of the entire picture which allows him to relax when he can. Kris' father passed away several years ago, but his mom and sister and brother and their families get along well and see each other as often as time permits.

On Rita's side, her family is also a warm group, and her sister Priscilla is a well-known star. She is the other half of the popular duo, "Booker T. and Priscilla." (Yes, Booker T., of "Booker T. and the MGs.") It was he who arranged Rita's 1977 hit, "Higher and Higher." Rita's father is a Baptist minister, and the family is Nashville-based.

Rita is especially aware of Kris' needs for a home base and feels that having this stability in his life has given him an added self-assurance. She is a tremendously supportive person, but by no means subordinate. When they met in 1972 in an airport, brought together by her manager, Kris immediately liked her because she was a "listener." She liked him because he was "fumbly-warm," as she put it. They were headed in different directions, he to do an interview with *Life* magazine and she to a recording session with her band, but Kris never gave that interview. Instead, he got off the plane in Memphis with Rita and they've been together ever since. They were married on August 19, 1973 by Rita's father.

There is an incredible warmth and understanding between these two which can be felt in their performances and in interviews. Kris says that a day doesn't go by that he doesn't feel grateful for the way things have

Rita Coolidge 1974   *Frank Edwards/Fotos International*

worked out in his life. He knows that most people never get as far as he has, and in every respect of his life, he feels fortunate.

It is no wonder, because for one thing, what he feels is most important is that there is a great deal of love and support in his family. Rita says she feels that she will live to a ripe old age because of the love in her family. She thinks of Kris' children, Tracy and Kris Jr., as her own. Their Casey is perhaps the single-most important factor in her life. Although her career is ever-growing, especially now after the tremendous success of her LP *Anytime . . . Anywhere*, she would drop it all if her daughter was suffering because of it. Casey is everything to them. In fact, because her heartthrob is Donny Osmond, Kris agreed to be a guest on *The Donny & Marie Show*. Now, that's devotion!

David Frost Show, 1973   *Chuck Pulin*

Of course, there were hard times: when Kris' movie career seemed as if it would eclipse his main concern — songwriting; when his drinking was getting in the way of his self-respect; when critics were panning him. He did pull himself through and, although Rita stood by him, she did not coddle him, but continued her career, giving support when needed, and always believing in him. Now, with his drinking days behind him, Kris says he feels

David Frost Show, 1973   *Chuck Pulin*   Radio City, NYC, 1977   *Chuck Pulin*

Rita Coolidge

Madison Square Garden, NYC   *Chuck Pulin*   Bottom Line, NYC, 1979   *Chuck Pulin*

better than he has in twenty years. Everything he has stands out so much more and he is able to appreciate it all doubly from a new perspective, because the good things in his life stuck with him. The mutual support between Kris and Rita is primary in making life so good.

This warmth and love is spread out in various ways. Kris feels that once he takes care of his own family, it is essential to spread his good fortune. He is active in raising funds for two organizations in particular. One is NORML, the National Organization for Reform of Marijuana Laws. He's been working for them for a few years now, although he says that the concerts which he does for NORML haven't really started bringing in money until recently. Kris has taped a radio spot for NORML which reminds people of the present laws and invites them to become involved in the organization, for the good of all concerned.

Kris also does work for the United Farm Workers. Again, he modestly says that he hasn't raised much money for them, but the fact that a well-known personality takes an active interest in the plight of the UFW surely does some good. Kris says that if he were to lose interest in this cause, he would be poorer for it.

Kris is one of those rare celebrities who don't mind paying taxes. As long as it goes to the right places, he feels that it is only equitable that he pay them. He is not greedy to hang onto every last cent. This is obviously because the creature comforts Kris needs are all within his grasp — he has his family and his work.

Of course his work does get in the way of his friendships with certain people. His closest friends, Johnny Cash and Willie Nelson, are both active performers, and the times when they can get together are few and far between. As time goes on, perhaps their schedules will ease up a bit, and these talents can relax together more. Kris says that sometimes things get so hectic that you don't have time for old dear friends, but you're constantly bombarded with people who only want you because of who you are.

There are certain trappings of stardom which cannot be avoided. After concerts, young songwriters run backstage begging Kris to listen to their work. He's tired, exhausted, and drained. He may ask for a tape to take home and hear, but they usually want to be heard right then. It's an awkward situation for Kris, who can remember just how it was for him. On the one hand, so many of the people are really poor writers, and he feels it's

Rita Coolidge

Madison Square Garden, NYC   *Chuck Pulin*   Bottom Line, NYC, 1979 *Chuck Pulin*

Donna Summer and Rita Coolidge   UNICEF Show, 1979   *Chuck Pulin*

wrong to give them false hope. On the other hand, if you don't listen, you may miss some very good things. John Prine, for example, was one of those who was a true find. He forced Kris to listen to him, and he was right! He should not have been ignored.

Fame does take its toll on celebrities, and Kris is determined not to become a callous star. "You always hear about famous actors and big rock people bitchin' endlessly about payin' taxes and signin' autographs, well I think you got a responsibility NOT to be that way. I'll tell you when I felt put upon; when I was a janitor. Hell, I can rent a car now; I can go wherever I want on this earth; I send all my kids to college on just a few songs. You can't tell me I'm in worse shape 'cause I got big taxes and responsibilities. I do feel like a shithead signin' autographs; they always ask when you're hurryin' to a plane carryin' three bags and a guitar, but if you don't sign, you feel like more of a shithead."

It is this concern for people which characterizes Kris and which has been felt by all who see or hear him. He is, aside from being talented and attractive, a good man, a thinking man who's concerned about all aspects of life.

He constantly changes and works over his approaches to his work. For a while, he was on the road so much that he felt his songwriting was suffering. "I had all sorts of ideas but I never got the time to sit down and finish the songs. All of it's starting to take me too far away from what I really am — a writer." He says he knows his limitations as a performer, but not as a writer. Now, he wants to devote himself more and more to writing, as opposed to acting, and is considering getting into screenwriting. This would be an excellent outlet for Kris' creative abilities. Beginning with the first movie he made, he always had suggestions for improving the scripts and has always worked on characters' lines and story-lines. Recall *Pat Garrett and Billy the Kid* when Kris rewrote some of Dylan's lines so that he could better evoke Dylan's character. It would certainly be a new challenge for him to conceive a story and write it out, planning all the characterizations in his own vivid way. It will be exciting to see what he comes up with.

AWARDS FOR MUSIC

1970

Country Music Association's Song of the Year: *Sunday Mornin' Comin' Down*

Academy of Country Music, Song of the Year: *For the Good Times*

Nashville Songwriter Association, Songwriter of the Year

Grammy, to Ray Price as Best Male Vocalist for his recording of *For the Good Times*

1971

Grammy, Best Song of the Year: *Help Me Make It Through The Night*

Grammy, Sammi Smith as Best Female Vocalist for her recording of *Help Me Make It Through The Night*

Country Music Association, Best Single of the Year: Sammi Smith for *Help Me Make It Through The Night*

Nashville Songwriters Association, Songwriter of the Year

1973

Grammy, Kris and Rita for Best Group Performance: *From the Bottle to the Bottom*

Nashville Songwriters Association, Songwriter of the Year

DISCOGRAPHY

THE SILVER-TONGUED DEVIL AND I (1971) Mon Z 30679

The Silver-Tongued Devil and I	Billy Dee
Jody And The Kid	Good Christian Soldier
Breakdown (A Long Way From Home)	
Loving Her Was Easier (Than Anything I'll Ever Do Again)	
The Taker	The Pilgrim—Chapter 33
When I Loved Her	Epitaph (Black and Blue)

ME & BOBBY MCGEE (1971) Col PZ 30817
(formerly released as *Kristofferson*)

Me & Bobby McGee	
Blame It All On The Stones	
To Beat The Devil	
Best Of All Possible Worlds	
Help Me Make It Through The Night	
Law Is For The Protection Of The People	
Just The Other Side Of Nowhere	For The Good Times
Casey's Last Ride	Duvalier's Dream
Darby's Castle	Sunday Mornin' Comin' Down

BORDER LORD (1972) Col PZ 31302

Josie
Burden Of Freedom
Stagger Mountain Tragedy
Border Lord
Somebody Nobody Knows

Little Girl Lost
Smokey Put The Sweat On Me
When She's Wrong
Gettin' By, High And Strange
Kiss The World Goodbye

JESUS WAS A CAPRICORN (1972) Mon KZ 31909

Jesus Was A Capricorn
Nobody Wins
It Sure Was (Love)
Enough For You

Help Me
I'm Sorry Too
Jesse Younger

Give It Time To Be Tender
Out Of Mind Out Of Sight
Sugar Man
Why Me

FULL MOON (1973) A & M Sp 4403

Hard To Be Friends
It's All Over
I Never Had It So Good
From The Bottle To The Bottom
Take Time To Love
Tennessee Blues

Part Of Your Life
I'm Down
I Heard The Bluebirds Sing
After The Fact
Loving Arms
Songs I'd Like To Sing

SPOOKY LADY'S SIDESHOW (1974) Mon PZ 32914

Same Old Song
Broken Freedom Song
Shandy (The Perfect Disguise)
Star Spangled Bummer
   (Whores Die Hard)
Lights of Magdala
I May Smoke Too Much

One For The Money
Late Again (Gettin' Over You)
Stairway To The Bottom
Rescue Mission
Smile At Me Again
Rock And Roll Time

BREAKAWAY (1974) Mon PZ 33278

Lover Please   Slow Down
We Must Have Been Out Of Our Minds
Dakota (The Dancing Bear)
What 'Cha Gonna Do
The Things I Might Have Been

Rain
Sweet Susannah
I've Got To Have You
I'd Rather Be Sorry
Crippled Crow

WHO'S TO BLESS AND WHO'S TO BLAME (1975) Mon PZ 33379

The Year 2000 Minus 25
If It's All The Same To You
Easy, Come On
Stallion
Rocket To Stardom

Stranger
Who's To Bless And Who's To Blame
Don't Cuss The Fiddle
Silver (The Hunger)

SURREAL THING (1976) Mon PZ 34254

You Show Me Yours	It's Never Gonna Be The Same Again
Killing Time	If You Don't Like Hank Williams
Prisoner	Stranger I Love
Eddie The Eunuch	Golden Idol
I Got A Life Of My Own	Bad Love Story

SONGS OF KRISTOFFERSON (1977) Col/Mon PZ 34687

The Silver-Tongued Devil And I   Me & Bobby McGee
Loving Her Was Easier (Than Anything I'll Ever Do Again)
Help Me Make It Through The Night   For The Good Times
Sunday Mornin' Comin' Down   You Show Me Yours
The Pilgrim—Chapter 33   Stranger I Love   Why Me
I Got A Life Of My Own   Who's To Bless And Who's To Blame

EASTER ISLAND (1978) Col JZ 35310

Risky Bizness   Sabre And The Rose   Bigger The Fool
How Do You Feel   Spooky Lady's Revenge   Lay Me Down
Forever In Your Love   Easter Island   The Fighter   Living Legend

NATURAL ACT (1978) A & M SP 4690

Blue As I Do   I Fought The Law   Number One
You're Gonna Love Yourself (In The Morning)
Loving Her Was Easier (Than Anything I'll Ever Do Again)
Back In My Baby's Arms   Please Don't Tell Me How The Story Ends
Hula Hoop   Love Don't Live Here Anymore   Silver Mantis

SINGLES DISCOGRAPHY

1971   *Loving Her Was Easier/Epitaph*
1971   *The Pilgrim/The Taker*
1972   *Josie/Border Lord*
1972   *Jesus Was A Capricorn/Enough For You*
1973   *Jesse Younger/Give It Time To Be Tender*
1973   *Why Me/Help Me*
1974   *I May Smoke Too Much/The Lights of Magdala*
1974   *Rain/What 'Cha Gonna Do*
1975   *Lover Please/Slow Down*
1975   *Sweet Susannah/We Must Have Been Out Of Our Minds*
1975   *Easy, Come On/Rocket To Stardom*
1975   *The Year 2000 Minus 25/If It's All The Same To You*
1976   *It's Never Gonna Be The Same Again/The Prisoner*